BECKI HAWKES

The Naming of Wings

SurVision Books

First published in 2022 by
SurVision Books
Dublin, Ireland
Reggio di Calabria, Italy
www.survisionmagazine.com

Copyright © Becki Hawkes, 2022
Cover image © Will Hawkes, 2022
Design © SurVision Books, 2022

ISBN: 978-1-912963-34-8

This book is in copyright. No part of this publication may be reproduced, stored in a retrieval system, or transmitted in any form or by any means without the prior permission in writing from the publisher.

Acknowledgements

Grateful acknowledgement is made to the editors of the following, in which some of these poems, or versions of them, originally appeared:

Perhappened, Brittle Star, Rust + Moth, Little Stone Journal, Lunate Fiction, Wrongdoing Magazine, Crow & Cross Keys, Ink Sweat & Tears, Selcouth Station, The Madrigal and *The Shore.*

CONTENTS

Banquet	5
Even as I take the photo, it is dying	6
Plant-based	8
Apple lover	10
Hidden teeth	12
Tower Hill	14
Red	16
Park run	18
Dreamt of a beach	20
Between the trees	22
Things that will never fossilise	24
Coat weather	26
Some boys terrify marine creature (6)	28
Cemetery park love song	30
Peacock, Orange Tip, Red Admiral, Holly Blue	32
Rival	34
The Earth gods are so small	36
The black and red day-flying moth	37
Myths and legends of the London parks	38
River run	40

Banquet

But yes I have always had eels, always loved
the way they make each space their own, scrunch
and slip between the smallest walls of my heart, rest
in Mesozoic slumber, long fossilised spines
slow dancing in their tank of rock. They have eaten

every single one of me, eaten the little girl
who combed the beach for shells, the shuffling teen
who hid her body from the sun, the cautious crinkled
woman who longed to dive with tigers. Today
they will eat the world, swallow everything, turn it

to glittering ocean soup, flour thickened gold and green
as a forest in summer, navy dark as an ancient gullet
and today I feel myself uncurving with them.
Widen, jaws! I am the Queen of the Eels
and I am ready to lose everything, again and again

and again. I think of my paddling years, how often
I'd wake crying, my body crushed against sweat-stained
land mammal bulk. I called that love but eels
have no time for tenderness. With them
I am packing a suitcase, wriggling my torso free

and taking the early train, pouring myself into waves
and waves of surging morning. With them
it is always dinner time. With them
it is always goodbye. I lie back, let the water
cover me, taste ships and salt and starfish, wait

for my soft yellow gills to open

Even as I take the photo, it is dying

Even as I take the photo, it is dying. Music
from a nearby flat seeps into the park
heat-soaked beats that make me think

of *getting ready*: the slow ritual of it
the skin-tight Primark bodycon, foundation
oil pastel thick on chins and foreheads, the taste

of Smirnoff Ice on our lips, alcohol
softened by sugar, the way we nonchalantly knew
we'd be desired. In the long light evening of today

I lean closer to the Comma that does not know
that I am taking its photo, that does not know
it is resting on the exact same metal fence

I saw another Comma bask on last summer,
and another the summer before that. Even the angle
of the wings is the same: the way it spreads them

wide and proud as sails, a kite in miniature
before it's off and airborne, darting up
to places I can only dream of:

where scalloped orange wings touch orange sky
and tree tops shimmer in cloudless electricity.
The mid-August weather holds

everything like a temple as my hands
sit on the fence with the missing butterfly
lightly brush against the absence

and my body softens in the sun, tells me
that it would like to fall in love again,
says that it thinks we could do it

Plant-based

I try not to bring it up but you're asking anyway
aggressively
if this is some kind of fad

and a knotted clutch of chicken legs
sprout up inside me, scrunched stars on stalks
that flail, pale yellow and scared

then run like hell, wheeling round
and round my skinless heart

as I grasp helplessly for facts, deflections
something irrefutable about climate change.

The truth? I was in his flat. He'd been drinking,
didn't really have a recipe

when he put me on the counter
and pulled out all my pliant feathers
one crass handful at a time.

I spat out my own stomach. Didn't move

as he slimed me, smeared me, made me
into a thing without a face. I don't know
the exact temperature or how long it took.

The next day I ate an apple and went to work
but just last year
a man on the London Underground
tried to eat me. I stood very still
as he latched on then quietly gnawed

my left arm. My face was hot
and I knew that if I didn't get off at the next stop
I would be gone completely, nothing left

but dog chews, tattered scraps
still carefully gripping the rail.

I'm explaining it badly. I'm not explaining it at all

but there is a canal inside me, a thick wet commute
where sawn-off beaks collect and bob in blood.
They have such small tongues

and I have no words
for all the eaten things, for all the things
that never get a say, that cannot speak

Apple lover

My favourite kind of apple? I place my palm
against your hair, press until both of us are anointed
with apple, crushed close, held

by the scent of the green apple
shampoo you started using
after I told you how the right apple

can throw you off completely, burst new buds
in your mouth, make you bleed, sweat, pray
for each torn crisp hit of sugar, squeezed out

by your very own teeth. I love
the hand-sized promise of them. I love Braeburn, Jazz,
Granny Smith. I once saw five Red Admirals, wings vivid as hearts

drink from the same fallen Bramley,
saw their long tongues, dreamed I could feast too

because it's been years
since it happened, and I don't talk about it much
but when I do

I always end by explaining how I lay there all night
then got up, took an apple from his fridge,
dressed myself and went to work. I used to think

that apple was a sign of me not functioning properly
blanking everything out, but now I suspect

my body simply knew what it needed before I did
made a choice to sustain itself, understood
there would be years of Russets, Galas, Pippins

my life ripening to now, to grabbed fistfuls of your apple hair
to all of me poured into yes. Because at first

when I tried
I'd see only his face, see myself flopped and useless,
letting him do it. But with you? With you

I only picture the apple. I've recombed the past,
I'm watching myself in honey-lit, crumble-sweet flashback
as I step out of his flat, apple in hand, sun on my face

and the street outside is not that street anymore
but an orchard, trees bowed to late summer

heat tumbled asleep in their arms. I am young, I am 21,
I am not looking back, I am
raising the apple to my mouth and walking on through the trees

and an entire green gold apple-flavoured universe
is shouting yes, you've got this, you'll be fine, stay alive
take a bite, take a bite, take a bite

Hidden teeth

Lick off the last bit
he says

and I do, though the way
it has gone cold and thick

makes me want to gag.

The word *slut*

is slippery, almost translucent
if you say it right

it is combed pearls
and languid curls of sea foam

it is a well-planned smile
that heats your tubes
as you muscle it out

it is a snail at night
on rain-sluiced bricks

inching its soft shape
into the smoked wet city
cell by cautious cell

scraping in moss
and shelled petals of beetle

feeding on stone

with all its hidden teeth

Tower Hill

This is our running route. This is ours:
two flights down, loop across the street

and then the river, the city
held, lost, held in it
our trainers carrying

all the light bones of our feet,
slapping them hard against the street
till they ache, spring, chant

that it is really our veins
we have in common:
leech-wet and elastic, rooting

across wild lamp trees
the Tesco Express, the fume pink sky

then throat-and-eye sweet Tower rosemary
livid ghosts of Barbary lions. I tell you how

the night before her execution
Katherine Howard
practiced carefully with the block

made sure she'd lay her neck
correctly, die just so

not drown in her own botched cords.
You've seen my wrist:

tattooed star ripped like paper
a fat long worm of a scar

but in London night
a healed star is good as new
necks unsnap, rolled heads turn tail

queens grow old and veins
are sealed and giddy with blood
channelling everything, sailing it back

to selfish, shuddering hearts

Red

Is your red
the same as my red?
Watching you

watching this painting

I am suddenly
flared soprano electric
parched mad needling desperate

for your red.

I don't know much
about art
but I know I like this painting:

I like how all of it is red
how its long smooth walls hum
and merge with its broad-brushed core

how we stand so close
we see each pucker and crater
each cooled-lava bubble lick
then step back so it eats us whole.

I like the way it is a painting of nothing
but red
how it breathes so many reds
how it makes red everything

and I like how I am suddenly sure
you are seeing the same red
I see

but even more of it:
your red-flecked air singing
each note strummed chaos on razored sun
each atom never ever still
yet still
miraculously obediently red

with you
I could talk about red for hours
drink red coffee, eat red sandwiches
in the red park, count the red swans
lie under this red lake of clouds

drown all day in your red red eyes

Park run

Google Maps
makes birds of us all, makes
this small spare triangle of green

between the main road, the houses
and the tube line
into something easily scrolled past, lost —

but I am human-sized now, have found
the air inside the air, driven
my trainers into the hard path, the wet mud

moved my body through fumes and sycamores,
over bridges and plague pits, spun

wide runner's loops
round the children on tricycles,
the double prams, the scooters, the man

who clasps a Costa with both hands
like a private prayer or tiny
love-squeezed rodent, like the last warm milk

in the universe. The skies here
don't go out without a fight:

make mirrored towers swell
with heatless colour, anoint cranes, turn the
bark on winter trees

to fragile copper skin

for a full four holy minutes –

and now the train screams past
one hard rushed dance of yellow squares

and this dying Wednesday
is awake with parakeets
exhilarating neon and familiar

Dreamt of a beach

that was covered in dead sharks, each one
planted upright in the sand, tails buried,
bodies shrivelled and grey, fins
flopped and useless in the sun. My brother
and I walked among them, looking for
one particular species (I could not remember
its name). We were both crying. The day was
very close and still. We were there for hours
but neither of us ever saw the sea.

We were looking for
one particular species. I could not remember
its name but I knew
that when I saw it, the word
would swim into my skull, fluid and predatory
and alive. We were both crying

but that was the only water. The day was
very close and still. We walked for hours

and we were looking for something
but there were only
salted bodies, shrivelled and grey, fins
flopped and useless in the sun.

I could not remember
its name

and then I could not remember.

Neither of us ever saw the sea.

Between the trees

After they were finished
they left me in the woods

and there are only trees now:
white birches, owl brown grooves between

each pathway out
a passage further in.

Some days
I am so hungry I eat the scared things
the velvet skin, the inquisitive mammalian skulls.

Their outraged little hearts flicker
against the roof of my mouth
pulse in my gullet, sleep in my acid.

Floppy crops of mushrooms
tug in all my torn holes, bleed weakly
when I pluck them out

and I am a hut
on tensed yellow chicken feet
an oven that yawns with bones.

Other days
I turn cunning, snout out
the cool forest berries

splatter my rose and nipples
with their juice

let my lips grow fat
inviting

them all back in: the lost prince
the huntsman, the handsome wolf.

Most don't make it
and those that do
say that they were lucky

but there is no luck
there is only me now

scabbed and crowned in lichen.

Only I decide

Things that will never fossilise

Knew from the start how his dig would look:
lost threads of pyjamas gobbled up
by earth and insects, the skull and neck
yanked back in a crescent of pain.

Today he says he can't get up
refuses to move from the sodden sheets.
Try coffee, I say at last (he always
liked his coffee first thing). Twin cups
from the same pot, the heat seeping
into our palms like the first broken cries of an orchestra
stretching its metal. Try just one sip

because outside the sky is loosening
baring

and there are so many things that will never fossilise:
that green river of sound as all the trees
let go at once

or the zig-zagged staccato of a first flight
a brave new raid against the sky. Think thousands
on thousands of wing cells, each one singing its colour
all hour long into the light

or the precise courtship rituals
of a never-named marine reptile, a dizzying reel
of eyes and nails and notes and tongues

and lungs and sweat and lashes
lapped up by the greedy salt.
I could never say them all –

and there's no time
for that. Only the bones live on
or if the soft parts by chance survive
they too will become hard and mineral
a negative kiss on an ancient tablet
a language that touches no one

but right now, there's the smell of it:
hot and bitter and tender, the way
he shifts up to drink and suddenly smiles
getting my name right for the last time

as we sit on the stripped bed
hearing birds, a far-away siren, music from a car
things that will never fossilise

Coat weather

I touch the thistledown: the cold
in its feathers licks me back and the last
Red Admiral of the year sits

at the summit of the almost-dead
buddleia, surveys the park ¬
like a superhero on a skyscraper

surveys her lost city, pulls back
her cape against the falling. I
watch her fly away, see summer die

through a pair of stained-glass wings
and know that later tonight, when I
get home from work so tired

and low that I will have nothing
but crisps and diet coke for dinner
I will put on my puffed coat and sit

on the balcony, let the bright trains
empty themselves into the night, turn
rails to metal violins, pierce the city

with their long industrial screams. I like
how even the emptiest carriages
feel swift and urgent, how they hurtle

fiercely into darkness, still aiming
for something, still diligently moving
things on. The only planet I can pick out

these nights is the planet Jupiter: I look for
it again and again, like a spell. I have not
felt this cold in a long while but my muscles

remember the moves, already know
how to tense and quiver and constrict
their long strings; make the most

of the heat they are already holding

Some boys terrify marine creature (6)

It takes you
to a shoreline in winter. The creature – soft-bodied,
bleeding out on to the sharp pebbles,
the cracked brown seaweed – is beached,
its fins dried and useless, its eyes begging
for help. It's alive, just, and its blood
is ocean blood, pale and grey as the sky. You want
to help it, roll it back to the nurse-soft water,
see it plump out into sudden grace, unfurl itself
like one of those flowering jasmine teas,
swim clean away –

but instead there are boys (some boys,
any boys). They have made a circle
and they are laughing, throwing stones
into the creature's opened skin.
Behind them, the ocean

sings a quiet song, not loud enough
to drown the high flayed pain that tastes like salt,
that comes in frightened waves, that will not stop –

but your brain, my love,
your canny, stalwart brain

can chew this out. There are always
routes out,
always more meanings than you think. Let it lap away
the horror, neatly behead
the boys, cut the terror in two

and you are fathoms deep now, have learned
the answer is to *oyster*, turn fear to pearl,
treasure your soft parts, grow yourself a new mineral shell
that opens only for the giving sea, its buried lights,
its tender green and purple sunken cradle.

NOTE: This poem was inspired by a crossword clue, first seen by the author in the magazine *The Big Issue*. The clue is solved by taking "some" of the phrase "boys terrify" – the "oys" of "boys" and the "ter" of terrify – to form the answer: the marine creature "oyster".

Cemetery park love song

Reading the headstones
feels like the polite thing to do
but I cannot keep my eyes

from the short-lived living. Green-veined
white butterflies flicker up like ghosts
between the graves and there are so many
more ladybirds than I expected. I feel
like I should feel something heavier:

all these nested bones and wars and moss-skinned
grey angels, stones studded with yellow snails
the names and dates going out
like muffled bells
but right now, in this forest of death
I do not want to think about dying. Right now

I am counting our ladybirds. Right now
I am Instagramming leaves. I take your hand in mine
and say it must be weird here at night
but what I am really saying
is that with you, death itself is just

a Victorian-themed adventure
playground: quaint and delicious;
well-scripted, almost fun. On my walk home

I find a piece of chalk on the bank near the railway
and draw our initials on a tree stump, joined
with a tiny heart. And yes part of me knows

that the chalk itself is a graveyard: fine layers
of tiny things, crushed limbs in a powder of time.
The other part pictures our ocean:
silver-bright as a beetle

and everything to swim for, all today.

Peacock, Orange Tip, Red Admiral, Holly Blue

Hello again, world: I am here
for the butterflies. My shins are bitten
and bloody, sucked raw by thorns and nettles

as I pull myself through knavish greenery
phone in hand, arms festooned with stickyweed
eyes on the bright speckled prize. Yesterday

I chased a tremulous white butterfly
across a road and through a car park, held
my breath when it finally rested, willed my eyes

into telescopes, begged them to show me
the underwing, whose pattern
would tell me exactly what it was. I've tried

to explain why the names matter: why logging
each species (and yes of course
there is an app for that)

is a small act of defiance, a fragile stand
against a breaking Earth, a broken us. In dreams
I track Large Tortoiseshells and Coppers

across oceans, watch them vanish
into light, wake up sobbing with loss. I am here
for the pollinated pauses, the jagged-edged moments

between the moments,
for Comma, after Comma, after Comma,

and I have seen people I love
unroot themselves, forget my name, forget
their own names, recognise nothing

and I have lain in a bed for a full weekend
cocooned in my own sweat and sorrow
wanting to die. But the first Brimstone of the year

never comes when I expect it: it is never
the preened garden, the tended quiet park

but the mess at the side of the road, fly-tipped
and unloved, where the first one dances out
and makes everything sweet and fierce as sun.

I call them like an army:
Peacock, Orange Tip, Red Admiral, Holly Blue
because this, now this is a love poem.

This is the naming of wings

Rival

My old boyfriend's old girlfriend
died when she was 19.
It was a hit and run. Afterwards

he wanted to die too
but I was there, and already knew

of plants that cling to coastal rocks
and sandbanks, anything that can grow
anywhere it can, those scattered colours

that are locked to cliffsides, drowned daily in salt
tugged and battered by stormwater
but do not unroot or let go. I knew

my job was to wait for him, to look
through photo after photo
of them together, say of course I understood
he loved her most. And yes

she was beautiful. A fist of nettles
in my throat. She was Tragedy
with a capital T, filmed in velvet lamplight
fattened on night berries, set to all the silken music

that ever made him cry. I held him
so carefully, for so many years, made him
a thousand seamless shirts, hid all
my jealous needlework, saw him break anyway
broke myself too –

but that was years ago. These days
are mine: I go to work, buy my coffee
watch the pigeons, pay my rent

let each new August sting and shriek and blaze
and snap and flower me, see flies
rise green as emeralds, cut my hair off
lie in meadows, dance by rivers, find her face.

Her eyes
meet the mouth of an old digital camera
and she has not changed, and yet
I barely know her. I barely know myself:

so world-bitten, rose-merry, crinkled up
in light and pity
and she so young –
so bloody fucking young I want to cry

The Earth gods are so small

It was mid-November and I was not expecting this
nor was I expecting so many of them: never so late
in the year or so late in the day. The first one I mistook
for a falling leaf but now they are everywhere: now they are
so close I can see the hairs on each green thorax, see each

needle tongue, could reach out and touch
if I wanted. The Earth gods are so small and their
wings drum the air as they descend at the end of everything
striped orange and scarlet and blue as the rapture, or speckled
forest brown or pale as moons, all of their bodies

singing and iridescent and urgent. I lie down on
the pavement, between the lamp posts and the parked
cars and the peeling old city trees and look
to my last sunset: to the high slim towers and restaurants,
to the stars and Jupiter lost in light. I tell the gods
that I am ready: feel my pores bloom and swell

with nectar and my bones shatter as the roots burst
through, piercing the concrete, binding me down
to the worm-fat Earth. I am screaming now, in pain and
delight and disintegration. I am twisting the stalks of me up
to the sky and the swarm. Eat me, I tell the gods. I am
truly ready. Everything now must be yours.

The black and red day-flying moth

When I was the last person alive on the Earth it was
strange at first: I cried all through the night until there was
no water left in me at all. I fell asleep, at last, and when I
woke it was pale and grey and raining and I held my dry
tongue out to taste the cloud. The sun came, slowly and
uncertainly, and with it the heat and the small things: the
black and red day-flying moth, wings pressed to a crumpled
heart, that crawled out from the deep roots where it had spent
the night and climbed to the top of a wild grass stem, ready
to take warmth from a star. I watched it sit there for almost
half an hour, the drops still wet on its wings, everything around it
fragile and shimmering and not quite solid, and took 47
pictures of it with my phone, even though I knew no one would
ever see them but myself. I heard voices, then: someone shouted
my name and the ground trembled and I knew that I had been
found; that I was no longer the only one left. I am not saying
I wasn't grateful, or happy, or relieved. But the disturbance
startled the moth into flight: made it pull itself up and away
and away, until the strings of my eyes could no longer reach it
or see where it had gone, or might go, or be again.

Myths and legends of the London parks

Pig tree is in Green Park. The legend goes
that a man once saw a woman under it
who was so ugly

he killed her on the spot. They say now
that all men who sit under the tree
are overcome by terror. Women

can lie there for hours, their bodies
held by peeled green light and feel
the same as usual. Rage and trepidation

hang so soft in the boughs above. The
leaves sing a warning, a lullaby
an elegy and a spell. What else

do you want to know? The pelicans
of St James's Park are a part of
London's history. They have lived there

for millions of years and the biggest one
is older than Britain itself. Her beak
is a long stone sword and an ancient

Mesozoic ship, a hull that has devoured
lost oceans. Years ago she drank
sharks and ammonites and writhing

silver-scaled ichthyosaurs
then swallowed nine thousand
soft lithe jellyfish to soothe

her salt-burned throat. Each of her legs
is as tall as the Shard and every time
she does something unexpected, like

eat a pigeon, or overturn an ice cream stand
or raise all the ghosts from the lakes
the newspapers use the same picture:

the one where she looks so angry
she could kill (a man was trying
to feed her. A man crossed the line

and stood too close). Her wings
stretch wide as summer skies along
the river, wide as the imaginary arms

we wrap around all the lost girls.
These days most Londoners
don't know the real story. Some say

the man died of fright, and that he
is the one we should feel sorry for. Some
say the tree was cut down. Only a few

could tell you her real name

River run

But what is this thing in me, that is not like me
at all but shrugs, laughs, says oh well
there will always be rivers: come run them
faster and faster? You cannot
cry here, because here, here
is a Buddleia, purple as heaven, laced
to the wall by the road. Search it, now
search it for butterflies. Search it again:
they are nestling in dark coiled
branches and scented spires, they are hiding
all over the city, in the light on the Thames
in parks and on towers and outside hospital windows
in tube station gardens and planted green graveyards
and benches for dead married couples, grieved and gone
but beloved and beloved and beloved,
they are beating their papery river wings, thriving
on pattern, finding the source. Today a Skipper
spiced orange and small as the top of my thumb
is caught in a sudden downpour, just as I pause
for breath, and I cannot help but hold out
my hand, lock my fingers into an umbrella
shield it from the violent air –
but this is a canny and weather-wise
insect, that already knows
to inch down the stem of the reed, to
hide under damp grasses, soften its shape
to leaf-secret littleness, fold undercover
say *tell us the worst, then,*
wait for the gap
in the sky

Selected Poetry Titles Published by SurVision Books

Seeds of Gravity: An Anthology of Contemporary Surrealist Poetry from Ireland
  Edited by Anatoly Kudryavitsky
  ISBN 978-1-912963-18-8

Invasion: An Anthology of Ukrainian Poetry about the War
  Edited by Tony Kitt
  ISBN 978-1-912963-32-4

Noelle Kocot. *Humanity*
  (New Poetics: USA)
  ISBN 978-1-9995903-0-7

Marc Vincenz. *Einstein Fledermaus*
  (New Poetics: USA)
  ISBN 978-1-912963-20-1

Helen Ivory. *Maps of the Abandoned City*
  (New Poetics: England)
  ISBN 978-1-912963-04-1

Tony Kitt. *The Magic Phlute*
  (New Poetics: Ireland)
  ISBN 978-1-912963-08-9

John W. Sexton. *Inverted Night*
  (New Poetics: Ireland)
  ISBN 978-1-912963-05-8

Alison Dunhill. *As Pure as Coal Dust*
  (Winner of James Tate Poetry Prize 2020)
  ISBN 978-1-912963-23-2

Aoife Mannix. *Alice under the Knife*
  (Winner of James Tate Poetry Prize 2020)
  ISBN 978-1-912963-26-3

Tony Bailie. *Mountain Under Heaven*
  (Winner of James Tate Poetry Prize 2019)
  ISBN 978-1-912963-09-6

Michelle Moloney King. *Another Word for Mother*
  (New Poetics: Ireland)
  ISBN 978-1-912963-31-7

Matthew Geden. *Fruit*
  (New Poetics: Ireland)
  ISBN 978-1-912963-16-4

Afric McGlinchey. *Invisible Insane*
  (New Poetics: Ireland)
  ISBN 978-1-9995903-3-8

Charles Borkhuis. *Spontaneous Combustion*
  (Winner of James Tate Poetry Prize 2021)
  ISBN 978-1-912963-30-0

Ciaran O'Driscoll. *Angel Hour*
  ISBN 978-1-912963-27-0

Tim Murphy. *Mouth of Shadows*
  ISBN 978-1-912963-29-4

George Kalamaras. *Through the Silk-Heavy Rains*
  ISBN 978-1-912963-28-7

Order our books from http://survisionmagazine.com/bookshop.htm